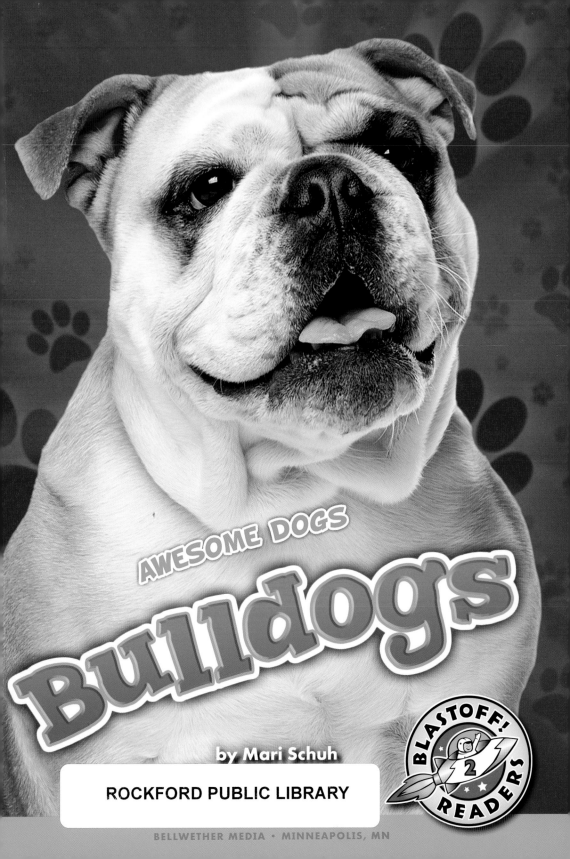

AWESOME DOGS

Bulldogs

by Mari Schuh

BLASTOFF!
2
READERS

BELLWETHER MEDIA • MINNEAPOLIS, MN

Note to Librarians, Teachers, and Parents:

Blastoff! Readers are carefully developed by literacy experts and combine standards-based content with developmentally appropriate text.

Level 1 provides the most support through repetition of high-frequency words, light text, predictable sentence patterns, and strong visual support.

Level 2 offers early readers a bit more challenge through varied simple sentences, increased text load, and less repetition of high-frequency words.

Level 3 advances early-fluent readers toward fluency through increased text and concept load, less reliance on visuals, longer sentences, and more literary language.

Level 4 builds reading stamina by providing more text per page, increased use of punctuation, greater variation in sentence patterns, and increasingly challenging vocabulary.

Level 5 encourages children to move from "learning to read" to "reading to learn" by providing even more text, varied writing styles, and less familiar topics.

Whichever book is right for your reader, Blastoff! Readers are the perfect books to build confidence and encourage a love of reading that will last a lifetime!

This edition first published in 2016 by Bellwether Media, Inc.

No part of this publication may be reproduced in whole or in part without written permission of the publisher. For information regarding permission, write to Bellwether Media, Inc., Attention: Permissions Department, 5357 Penn Avenue South, Minneapolis, MN 55419.

Library of Congress Cataloging-in-Publication Data
Schuh, Mari C., 1975- author.
 Bulldogs / by Mari Schuh.
   pages cm. – (Blastoff! Readers. Awesome Dogs)
 Summary: "Relevant images match informative text in this introduction to bulldogs. Intended for students in kindergarten through third grade"–Provided by publisher.
 Audience: Ages 5-8.
 Audience: K to grade 3.
 Includes bibliographical references and index.
 ISBN 978-1-62617-304-0 (hardcover : alk. paper)
 1. Bulldog–Juvenile literature. 2. Dog breeds–Juvenile literature. I. Title. II. Series: Blastoff! Readers. 2, Awesome Dogs.
 SF429.B85S38 2016
 636.72–dc23
                                    2015034238

Printed in the United States of America, North Mankato, MN.

Table of **Contents**

Bulldogs are short, wide dogs. They **waddle** when they walk.

4

This **breed** may look mean or tough. But bulldogs are friendly and gentle.

Bulldogs have **stocky** bodies. They are heavy for their size.

They weigh between 40 and 50 pounds (18 to 23 kilograms).

muzzle

Bulldogs have short **muzzles** and big heads. **Wrinkles** cover their faces.

They have **droopy** mouths. Their bottom teeth often stick out!

Bulldogs have smooth, short **coats**. Their fur is usually white, **fawn**, or red.

piebald   fawn   brindle

Some have patterned coats
like **piebald** or **brindle**.

History of Bulldogs

Bulldogs first came from England. They may have been **bred** from mastiffs and pugs.

England

N
W E
S

In the 1200s, people bred
bulldogs to fight bulls. That is
how the breed got its name.

By the early 1800s, the dogs
no longer fought bulls.

People then bred bulldogs to be gentle and calm. They became popular pets!

Today, bulldogs are part of the
American Kennel Club.

The breed is in its **Non-Sporting Group**.

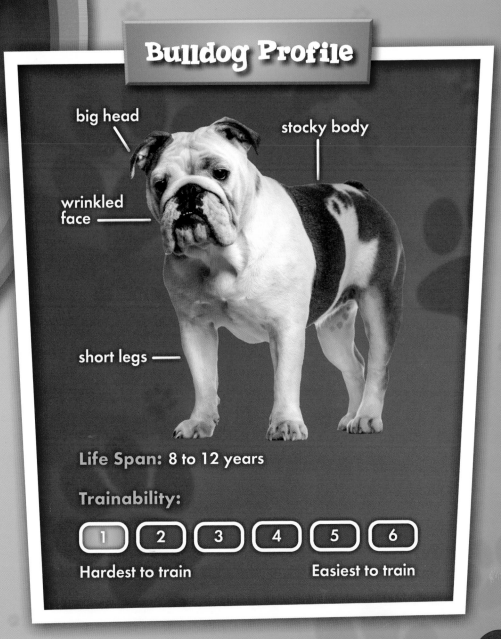

Bulldog Profile

big head

stocky body

wrinkled face

short legs

Life Span: 8 to 12 years

Trainability:

1 | 2 | 3 | 4 | 5 | 6

Hardest to train

Easiest to train

Easygoing Dogs

Bulldogs stay mostly indoors. This breed cannot breathe well in hot weather.

But they need some exercise.
They can go for short walks
in cool weather.

Bulldogs are **easygoing**.
They are friendly with strangers.

These dogs like to cuddle and sit on people's laps. They love getting face rubs!

Glossary

American Kennel Club—an organization that keeps track of dog breeds in the United States

bred—purposely mated two dogs to make puppies with certain qualities

breed—a type of dog

brindle—a solid coat color mixed with streaks or spots of another color

coats—the hair or fur covering some animals

droopy—saggy and hanging down

easygoing—calm and free of worries

fawn—a light brown color

muzzles—the noses and mouths of animals

Non-Sporting Group—a group of dog breeds that do not usually hunt or work

piebald—a coat of white fur with patches of another color

stocky—having a solid, heavy body

waddle—to take short steps and sway from side to side

wrinkles—lines in skin or fur

To Learn More

AT THE LIBRARY

Barnes, Nico. *Bulldogs*. Minneapolis, Minn.: Abdo Kids, 2015.

Bodden, Valerie. *Bulldogs*. Mankato, Minn.: Creative Education, 2014.

Riggs, Kate. *Bulldogs*. Mankato, Minn.: Creative Education, 2016.

ON THE WEB

Learning more about bulldogs is as easy as 1, 2, 3.

1. Go to www.factsurfer.com.

2. Enter "bulldogs" into the search box.

3. Click the "Surf" button and you will see a list of related web sites.

With factsurfer.com, finding more information is just a click away.

Index